# THE SCIENCE BOOK OF SOUND

**Project Editor** Linda Martin
**Art Editor** Peter Bailey
**Designer** Mark Regardsoe
**Photography** Dave King
Created by Dorling Kindersley Limited, London

Printed in the United States of America

ISBN 0-15-365404-X

1 2 3 4 5 6 7 8 9 10   036   96   95   94   93   92

# THE SCIENCE BOOK OF SOUND

Neil Ardley

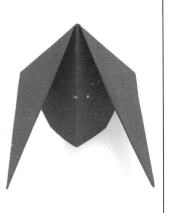

Harcourt Brace Jovanovich, Publishers

Orlando    San Diego    Chicago    Dallas

## About the Author

Neil Ardley has written a number of innovative nonfiction books for children, including *The Eyewitness Guide to Music*. He also worked closely with David Macaulay on *The Way Things Work*. In addition to being a well-known author in the fields of science, technology, and music, he is an accomplished musician who composes and performs both jazz and electronic music. He lives in Derbyshire, England, with his wife and daughter.

# Contents

# What is sound?

Sounds are nothing more than tiny movements of the air. You cannot feel these movements, but your ears detect them and your brain turns them into sounds that you can recognize. Every day you hear sounds made by people, animals, wind, and machines. The sounds you make with your voice allow you to communicate with other people. Animals also use sounds as a way of communicating with one another.

### Sound signals
We often use sounds as signals. Blowing a whistle in a game can mean "stop" or "go."

### Sea songs
Whales in the ocean "sing" to each other. One whale can hear the call of another as far as 800 kilometers (500 miles) away!

### The speed of sound
The sound of this balloon bursting does not take long to travel through the air. Sound moves through air at a speed of 340 meters (1,115 feet) per second.

## Sound pictures

The picture on this screen shows an unborn baby inside its mother. The picture was made using sounds that are too high-pitched for us to hear. These sounds are called "ultrasound."

## Making music

Music is great fun. You can make musical sounds with homemade instruments like these.

⚠️ This is a warning symbol. It appears within an experiment next to a step that requires caution. When you see this symbol, ask an adult for help.

**Be a safe scientist**
Follow all the instructions carefully and always use caution, especially with glass, scissors, and electricity.

Never put anything into your ears, eyes, or mouth. Remember that loud noises can bother other people. Please be considerate when doing these experiments.

# Squawkers and screechers

You can make some strange sounds without using your voice. All you need is a piece of plastic or a straw. With practice, these can sound like the cries of wild animals!

**1** Hold the strip of plastic tightly between your thumbs and the heels of your hands.

**2** Blow hard across the strip. It makes a loud screeching sound.

*Try bending your thumbs as you blow.*

**1** Press one end of the straw flat. Cut the sides to form a point.

*Keep the end of the straw flat.*

*Try two or more straws at once. Cut them to different lengths.*

**2** Put the pointed end of the straw in your mouth and blow hard. Out comes a weird squawk!

# Balloon sounds

Make a loud shrieking noise with a balloon and you will see how rapid movements, or "vibrations," make sound.

**You will need:**

Balloon pump

Balloon

**1** Pump up the balloon. Pinch the neck to stop the air escaping.

**2** Grip the neck of the balloon and stretch it. The balloon makes a sound as the air escapes.

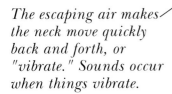

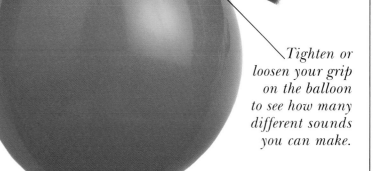

*The escaping air makes the neck move quickly back and forth, or "vibrate." Sounds occur when things vibrate.*

*Tighten or loosen your grip on the balloon to see how many different sounds you can make.*

**Human sounds**
Vocal cords in your throat vibrate and make sounds as the air from your lungs flows over them. Your mouth and lips form these sounds into words.

# Sound detector

How do we hear the sounds around us? You can make a plastic drum and see how it detects sound. Your ears detect sounds in the same way.

**You will need:**

Rubber band

Plastic bowl

Saucepan

Piece of plastic

Uncooked rice

Scissors

Large spoon

Tape

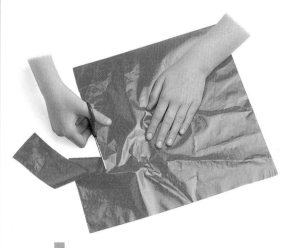

**1** Cut the piece of plastic so that it is a few inches bigger than the top of the bowl.

**2** Stretch the plastic tightly over the bowl and secure it with a rubber band.

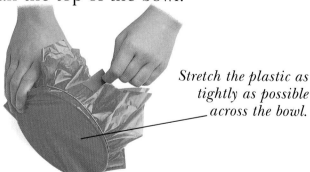

*Stretch the plastic as tightly as possible across the bowl.*

**3** Tape the plastic down to keep it taut. This is your drum.

**4** Sprinkle a few grains of rice on top of the drum.

**5** Hold the saucepan near the drum and hit it sharply with the spoon. The grains of rice jump up and down.

*When you hit the saucepan, it vibrates.*

*The sound travels through the air to the plastic drum, which also vibrates.*

*The vibrations cause the rice to jump.*

*If you look from the side, you can see the rice jumping up and down quite clearly.*

## Inside the ear

Inside each of your ears is a thin sheet of skin called the eardrum. Sounds are directed to your eardrum by your outer ear. When they reach the eardrum, it vibrates. The inner ear transforms these vibrations into signals that the brain then translates into the sounds you hear.

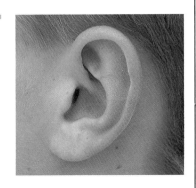

# Traveling sound waves

Sounds travel through the air by spreading out in invisible waves, similar to the ripples on a pond. These waves are called "sound waves." Fire a sound wave at a target and see sound waves in action.

**You will need:**

Thin plastic

Stiff paper

Cardboard tube

Strip of paper

Pencil

Scissors

Rubber band

Tape

**1** Use the tube to trace a circle on the piece of paper.

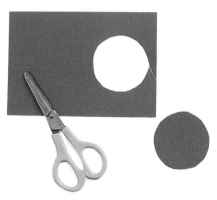

**2** Cut out the circle.

**3** Make a hole in the center of the circle with the pencil.

**4** Tape the circle firmly to one end of the tube.

**5** Fold the plastic over the other end of the tube, and secure it with the rubber band.

**6** Make a fold in the paper strip and tape one end to a flat surface so that the other end sticks up.

*The tap makes the air inside the tube vibrate and a sound wave travels down the tube.*

**7** Position the end of the tube so the hole is directly above the paper strip. Sharply tap the other end of the tube.

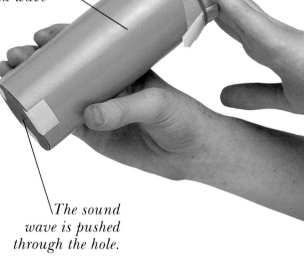

*The air moves back and forth as the sound wave passes, shaking the paper strip.*

*The sound wave is pushed through the hole.*

**Sliding snow**
A loud sound can cause an avalanche. The sound waves disturb the snow and start a mass of snow suddenly sliding down the mountain.

# Paper noisemaker

You can make a loud bang with just a sheet of paper! This will show you how a sudden movement can send a powerful sound wave rushing through the air. You can use your noisemaker to surprise and startle your friends.

**You will need:**

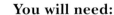

Sheet of paper about
30 x 40 cm (12 x 16 in)

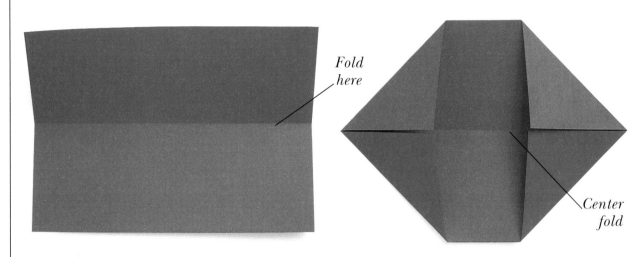

*Fold here*

*Center fold*

**1** Fold the longest edges of the paper together. Crease firmly, then unfold it.

**2** Fold down each of the four corners to the first center fold.

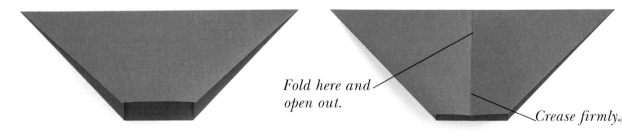

*Fold here and open out.*

*Crease firmly.*

**3** Fold the paper in half along the first center fold.

**4** Fold the paper in half again and then open it.

**6** Fold the paper back to make a triangle. The noisemaker is now ready.

**5** Fold down the two top corners.

**7** Grip the noisemaker firmly by the two top corners. Snap it down sharply with a quick flick of the wrist. You should hear a loud bang!

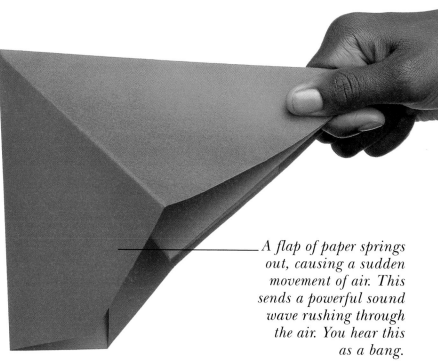

*A flap of paper springs out, causing a sudden movement of air. This sends a powerful sound wave rushing through the air. You hear this as a bang.*

### Thunderclap
In a thunderstorm, a flash of lightning makes a powerful sound wave spread out through the air. When this sound wave reaches our ears, we hear a thunderclap.

# Talking string

Besides traveling through air, sounds can also travel through objects. You can demonstrate this by making a simple telephone. This will show you how a tight string carries sound.

**You will need:**

Tape

Two rubber bands

Two pieces of tracing paper

String

Two paper clips

Pencil

Two cardboard tubes

**1** Fold a piece of tracing paper over one end of each tube. Attach it with a rubber band.

**2** Pull the paper tight and tape it securely.

*The vibrations of your friend's voice make the tube and string vibrate.*

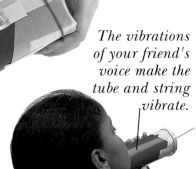

**3** Make a small hole in the center of both pieces of tracing paper.

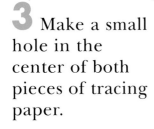

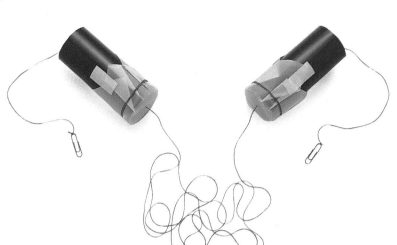

*The vibrating string makes your tube vibrate. You hear those vibrations as your friend's voice.*

**4** Thread the string through the holes in both tubes. Tie a paper clip to each end to prevent the string from slipping back through the hole.

*The vibrations travel swiftly along the tight string. The sound stops if the string is loose and cannot vibrate.*

**5** Use the tubes as a simple telephone. Hold one tube to your ear and listen while your friend speaks softly into the other tube.

**Prong notes**
Tapping the prongs of a tuning fork produces a soft musical note. But if you place the handle of the tuning fork on a hard surface, the note becomes louder. The vibrations of the fork travel into the surface, making it vibrate, too.

# Finding the beat

Can you hear a sound as faint as a heartbeat? By making a simple stethoscope you will find out how to make soft sounds louder.

**You will need:**

Scissors

Plastic tubing

Tape

Funnel

**1** Insert the funnel into the plastic tube and secure it with tape.

*Sound waves from the heart collect in the funnel. They travel along the tube to your ear.*

*Be careful not to stick the tube into your ear.*

**2** ⚠ Put the funnel against a friend's chest and hold the end of the tube to your ear. You will hear the low thud of the heart beating.

### Listening in

The stethoscopes doctors use have two tubes that allow them to use both ears to listen to sounds inside the body. The sounds they hear tell them whether or not parts of the body are working properly.

# Loud mouth

Can you make your voice louder without shouting? With just a sheet of paper and some tape, you can make a megaphone.

**You will need:**

Tape

Scissors

Large sheet of paper

**1** Roll the paper into a cone.

**2** Tape the edge of the rolled paper to secure it.

*The cone collects the sound waves of your voice and sends them forward.*

**3** Talk into the narrow end of the cone. Your voice sounds louder.

*The cone now collects sounds and directs them to your ear.*

**4** Now place the narrow end of the cone against your ear. You can hear soft sounds much more easily.

# Bouncing sound

Sometimes sound waves hit an object before they reach our ears. When this happens, the sound waves bounce back and we hear the sound as a reflection, or "echo." This experiment shows you how to bounce sound.

**You will need:**

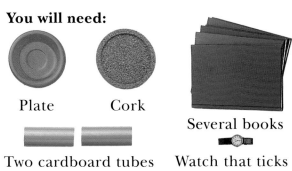

Plate        Cork        Several books

Two cardboard tubes    Watch that ticks

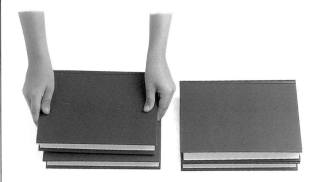

**1** Stack two piles of books. They must be the same height.

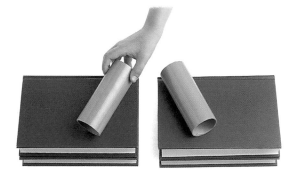

**2** Carefully lay the tubes on the books as shown above.

**3** Make sure that the watch is ticking.

**4** Place the watch just inside the end of one tube.

**5** Listen at the end of the other tube. You cannot hear the watch. Ask a friend to hold the plate near the far ends of the tubes. Now you can hear the watch.

*The sound waves bounce off the plate and travel through the second tube to your ear.*

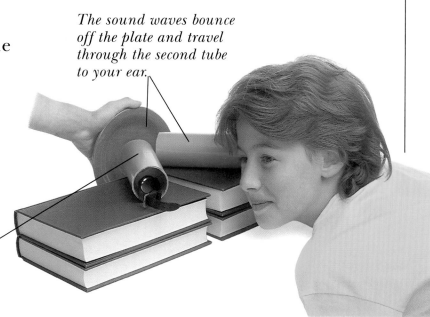

*Sound waves from the watch travel through the first tube.*

*The soft cork soaks up the sound waves.*

**6** Replace the plate with the cork. Now you cannot hear the watch.

**More things to try**
Try pieces of wood, metal, or cotton. Hard surfaces bounce sound, but soft surfaces do not.

## "Seeing" with sound
When they fly, bats make high squeaking sounds that bounce off objects in their path. These echoes tell the bats about the size and position of objects and allow them to find their way in the dark and catch flying insects.

# Plastic drum

How do musical instruments make sounds? Make a drum and see how to change its "pitch," or make the sound higher or lower.

**You will need:**

Rubber band

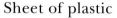
Pen

Sheet of plastic

Plastic bowl

*The skin of the drum and the air inside it vibrate to create a booming sound.*

**1** Fit the plastic over the bowl. Pull the plastic tight and secure it with the rubber band.

**2** Grip the plastic firmly to stretch it smoothly across the bowl. Strike it with the pen. It makes the sound of a drum.

*Tighten and relax your grip as you play. The note becomes higher and lower. The tighter the skin, the higher the pitch.*

**Talking drum**
The cords on this African drum change its pitch. Pressing them while striking the drum raises and lowers the pitch and produces sounds similar to someone talking.

# Simple shakers

Different percussion instruments produce various noises as you beat or shake them. You can make some shakers and see how different objects create sounds of different pitch.

**You will need:**

Scissors

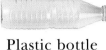
Plastic bottle

Paper clips

Colored tape

*Make sure the bottle is dry inside.*

**1** Put a few paper clips into the bottle. Screw on the cap firmly.

**2** Hold the bottle and shake it back and forth. The paper clips strike the sides of the bottle and produce a rattling sound.

*Shake with short flicks of the wrist.*

*Pasta*

*Dried peas*

*Pins*

*Uncooked rice*

*Marbles*

*Mustard seeds*

*Lentils*

**3** Collect other small objects and make more shakers with them. They all make different sounds.

**4** You can also decorate your shakers with strips of colored tape.

# Rubber guitar

Can you make music with rubber bands? By stretching the bands across a baking pan and plucking them, you can mimic the sound of a guitar and learn how string instruments work.

**You will need:**

Three coloring pens

Baking pan

Rubber bands of varying thickness

**1** Stretch the rubber bands lengthwise across the pan.

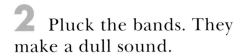

*The vibrations of the bands are muffled because they rub against the top of the pan.*

**2** Pluck the bands. They make a dull sound.

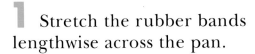

*The pens raise the rubber bands above the pan.*

**3** Now put a pen underneath the rubber bands at each end of the pan.

*The pitch of the notes depends on how fast the bands vibrate. Thin bands vibrate quickly and produce high notes.*

**4** Pluck the bands again. The sound is much clearer than it was before.

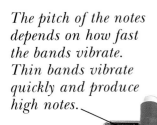

*Thick, heavy bands vibrate less quickly and produce low notes.*

*Vibrations pass through the pens to the pan. Most of the sound comes from the pan as it vibrates.*

**5** Press the third pen onto the bands. Slide it back and forth while you pluck the bands. The pitch of the notes changes.

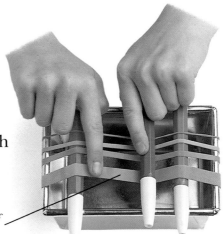

*The notes get higher as you shorten the vibrating part of each band.*

### String sounds
Guitar players press the strings with one hand and pluck them with the other. Pressing the strings changes the notes by making the vibrating parts shorter or longer.

# Bottle pipes

You can make music with a few bottles and some water. See and hear how different amounts of air vibrate and make different sounds.

**You will need:**

Food coloring

Water

Narrow-necked glass bottles

**1** Set the bottles in a line. You will need six or more bottles to make a tune.

*Gradually change the level of water in each bottle.*

**2** Pour a different amount of water into each bottle.

**3** Color the water to make the levels easier to see.

**4** Blow gently across the top of each bottle. Each one produces a different musical note.

*Blowing across the top of the bottle makes the air inside vibrate. Short columns of air vibrate more quickly than long columns of air.*

*You can change the water levels to create different notes and make a tune.*

*A long column of air makes a low note.*

*A short column of air makes a high note.*

**Pipe organ**
Each pipe in this huge organ sounds one note. When the organ is played, air is blown across holes at the base of each pipe, causing the column of air in the pipe to vibrate and produce a note. Together, these notes form music.

# Cardboard flute

Woodwind instruments, such as the flute, clarinet, and oboe, are pipes with holes in them. With just one cardboard tube you can make your own woodwind instrument that produces several notes.

**You will need:**

Cardboard tube

Drinking straw

Tracing paper

Pencil

Scissors

Tape

**1** Press one end of the straw flat. Cut the sides to make a point.

**2** Fold the tracing paper over one end of the tube and secure it with tape.

**3** Using the pencil, make a small hole in the center of the tracing paper.

**4** Carefully push the round end of the straw through the hole.

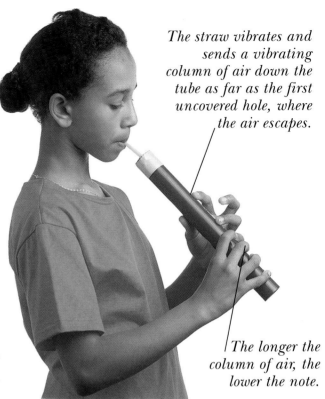

*The straw vibrates and sends a vibrating column of air down the tube as far as the first uncovered hole, where the air escapes.*

**5** With the pencil, make six holes along the length of the tube.

**6** Cover the holes with your fingers and blow into the straw. By moving your fingers on and off the holes, you can change the pitch of the note.

*The longer the column of air, the lower the note.*

## Bags of sound

To play the bagpipes, the player squeezes the bag, sending air into the pipes. The pipe with holes, or the "chanter," plays a tune. The other pipes each sound only one note.

**Picture credits**
(Abbreviation key: B=below, C=center, L=left, R=right, T=top)

Catherine Ashmore: 25BL; Clive Barda: 9BL; Dorling Kindersley: 22BL; Pete Gardner: 6BL, 6BR, 7CL, 11BR, 17BR; Robert Harding Picture Library: 13BL; The Image Bank: 15BL; Dave King: 6TL; NHPA/Trureo Nakamuta: 6CR; Stephen Dalton: 21BR; Science Photo Library/Alexander Tsiaras: 7TL; Chris Priest &

Mark Clarke: 18BL; Scottish Tourist Board: 29CL; Zefa: 27BL

**Picture research** Paula Cassidy and Rupert Thomas

**Production** Louise Barratt

Dorling Kindersley would like to thank Claire Gillard for editorial assistance; Mrs Bradbury, the staff and children of Allfarthing Junior School, Wandsworth,

especially Idris Anjary, Melanie Best, Benny Grebot, Miriam Habtesellasse, Alistair Lambert, Lucy Martin, Paul Nolan, Dorothy Opong, Alan Penfold, Ben Saunders, David Tross, and Alice Watling; Tom Armstrong, Michael Brown, Damien Francis, Stacey Higgs, Mela Macgregor, Katie Martin, Susanna Scott, Natasha Shepherd, and Victoria Watling.

*Cornerstones of Freedom*

# Ellis Island

R. Conrad Stein

**CP** CHILDRENS PRESS®

CHICAGO

Library of Congress Cataloging in Publications Data

Stein, R. Conrad.
Ellis Island / R. Conrad Stein.

  p. cm. — (Cornerstones of freedom)
  Summary: Describes the history, closing, and
restoration of the Ellis Islnd immigration center and
depicts the experiences of the immigrants who came to
Ellis Island at the turn of the twentieth century.
ISBN 0-516-06653-6
  1. Ellis Island Immigration Station (New York, N.Y.)—
History—Juvenile literature. 2. United States—
Emigration and immigration—History—Juvenile
literature. [1. Ellis Island Immigration Station (New
York, N.Y.)—History. 2. United States—Emigration and
immigration—History.] I. Title. II. Series.
JV6484.S74   1992
325.1'0973—dc20                                    91-33222
                                                   CIP
                                                   AC

A ship steamed into New York Harbor in 1905. Hundreds of excited immigrants crowded on deck. They spoke different languages, but this morning there was only one word on their lips— "America."

"There she is!" someone shouted.

The head and upstretched arm of the Statue of Liberty appeared above the morning mist. People pushed to the rail to get a better view. Mothers lifted their small children. A few people cried. Some knew the words written on the base of the great statue: "Give me your tired, your poor, Your huddled masses yearning to breathe free." All knew the Statue of Liberty welcomed them.

*The main building at Ellis Island in the early 1900s*

*Those who stayed in New York after passing through Ellis Island faced a huge, crowded, unfamiliar city.*

Almost in her shadow lay a tiny piece of land. This was Ellis Island, a giant processing center. Here an immigrant would either be allowed to enter the United States or refused and sent back to Europe. In many European languages, Ellis Island was called the "Isle of Tears."

If the immigrants were lucky, they passed through Ellis Island quickly. Then they found themselves on the busy streets of a confusing city where the people spoke a foreign tongue. Most of them had just a few dollars in their pockets. Many were farm folk who would have to learn how to live in the city. Most were uneducated. All would have to take backbreaking jobs for wages of ten to fifteen dollars a week.

Still, the immigrants flocked to America. During the first years of the twentieth century, nearly a million people a year passed through Ellis Island. Many came from Russia, Poland, Yugoslavia, southern Germany, Italy, and Greece. Frightened and confused, these brave immigrants left Ellis Island to enter a new life.

Why did so many millions uproot themselves from the Old World to face the hardships of life in America? That question can be answered in

*Immigrants waiting to be processed at Ellis Island, around 1900*

one word: hope. The people arriving at Ellis Island hoped, believed, and prayed they would find a better life in the United States. The overwhelming majority did.

From its beginnings, the United States has been a nation of immigrants. Only American Indians can truly call themselves "native Americans."

Historians usually divide American immigration into three time periods. The colonial period ran from the early 1600s to 1776. The period of "old" immigration stretched from 1776 to 1890. The "new" immigration began when millions came to America during the 1890s and early 1900s.

Most of the immigrants during the colonial period were English and Scottish. Colonies of German and Dutch settlers also arrived. A sorry chapter in American history occurred during this period as thousands of slaves were brought from Africa to the New World.

The period of "old" immigration was highlighted by the coming of more than two million Irish. Most of them crossed the Atlantic to escape what was called the Great Irish Potato Famine. The famine was caused by a plant disease that struck Ireland in the 1840s and made potatoes rot in the fields. Since the Irish people depended almost entirely on potatoes for food, most of the country was starving. One of the Irish immigrants who came to America during the potato famine was Patrick Kennedy. His great-grandson would become the thirty-fifth president of the United States.

After the American Civil War, thousands of German, Swedish, and Norwegian farmers came to the United States. They were attracted by free land given away under the Homestead Act. Also during this time, many Chinese settled on the West Coast. They worked on the railroads and in the mines.

Finally came the period of "new" immigration. Millions streamed to America to escape the

*These 1854 cartoons show an Irish immigrant on his way to America (left) and on his way back to Ireland (right) after having found fortune in the "land of opportunity."*

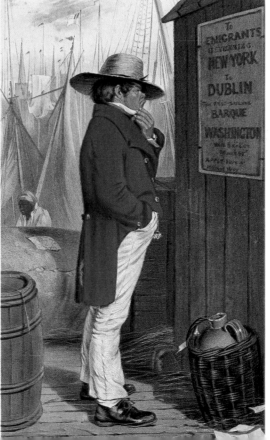

hopeless poverty and overpopulation of southern and eastern Europe. The mass migration of people from the Old World to the New World after 1890 was like a human flood. No other country in modern history had ever experienced anything like it.

The long journey for these new immigrants began deep in Europe. Exaggerated stories of wealth in the United States circulated freely among European peasants. America was often pictured as a Garden of Eden where poverty and hunger did not exist. "They used to tell us that the streets in the United States were paved with gold," said one woman who grew up in a Croatian village. "When I was a little girl I thought that all Americans were millionaires."

A more accurate picture of life in America came from letters from relatives who had already immigrated. "In my little village only the priest could read or write," one Italian immigrant remembered. "Whenever anyone got an "America letter" from an uncle or a cousin the whole village would gather at the church to hear the priest read it."

Usually the "America letters" told the truth about life in the United States. The work there was hard and the wages were small. Most immigrants lived in crowded apartments. Still, with enough hard work and a little luck, a person could eventually buy his own home and send his

*An immigrant family's apartment in New York City, about 1910*

children to school. A home of one's own! An
education for the children! Incredible, thought
the European peasants, who had lived in poverty
all their lives as had their fathers and their
grandfathers before them.

Penny by penny, families saved their money to
pay for the trip to America. Very often, the trip
cost too much for the whole family, so the father
went first. He would get a job and later send for
the family.

Sometimes parents would save their money
and send their oldest son or daughter to America.
When a European left his village to immigrate,

*Steerage quarters, usually in the lowest deck of a ship, were dark, dirty, and overcrowded.*

he usually left it for life. Never again would he see the people and the places he once loved. One teenager told of leaving his mother and father at a train station in a small Russian town. "When the train drew into the station my mother lost control of her feelings. As she embraced me for the last time her sobs became violent and Father had to separate us. There was a despair in her way of clinging to me which I could not understand then. I understand it now. I never saw her again."

When the immigrant arrived at a European

port city he soon learned a new word—steerage. "What is this steerage?" one immigrant asked another.

"It is the basement of the ship," came the reply.

The word *steerage* referred to that part of a ship kept for the passengers who pay the lowest fares. Usually steerage was in the lowest deck of a steamship. One passenger in 1903 wrote, "We climbed down to steerage by going down a narrow, steep stairway. It was dark and slippery. Once there, I saw people lying in bunks that were stacked up one on top of the other. The people did not have enough room to sit up in bed. The smell inside was terrible."

A steerage ticket to New York cost ten to fifteen dollars in 1910. It was the only ticket the immigrant could afford.

*Dutch children at Ellis Island in 1906*

Most steerage passengers had never even seen the ocean before, much less sailed on a ship. A Jewish immigrant from Russia said, "A storm hit us on the second night out in the Atlantic. I remember women were screaming, babies were crying, and dishes were falling out of the top beds and breaking on the floor. We all thought the end was near." Another remembered his horrible seasickness: "I couldn't get out of bed for two whole days."

But storms did not last forever, and the Atlantic crossing was not one long ordeal. On sunny days, people went up on deck. One of the

*On sunny days, steerage passengers came out of their cramped quarters and spent time on the open deck of the ship.*

immigrants might have an accordion. Others would sing. If the song was in a strange language, a person could still hum the tune. One young man had never met anyone from outside his own village before, but on board ship . . . "I asked a girl to dance with me, but she did not speak Polish. I used sign language and pretty soon we were dancing all over the deck. I couldn't believe I was dancing with a girl who I couldn't speak with, not one word."

The Atlantic crossing took about three weeks.

At New York Harbor, the steamship first docked at Manhattan. There the first-class and cabin-class passengers got off the ship. The immigrants in steerage waited. Then a ferryboat tied alongside and the immigrants climbed aboard. Their next stop was Ellis Island.

Ellis Island is about one mile south of Manhattan. It was once used by early Dutch settlers as a picnic ground. Immigrants used to come through a center called Castle Garden at the tip of Manhattan. But after 1885, when the stream of immigrants was becoming a flood, the federal government decided to build a new

*Before Ellis Island was built, immigrants arriving in New York came through Castle Garden, at the southern tip of Manhattan.*

*Immigrants crowd the deck of a ship to get their first look at New York Harbor and the Statue of Liberty.*

center. Ellis Island opened in 1892. Before its doors were closed in 1954, more than 16 million people passed through its great hall.

As the ferryboat, jammed with immigrants, drew near Ellis Island, many people began to worry. They had heard stories of immigrants who had been held there for many days. Others had been sent back to Europe. Would it happen to them? Had they saved their money for what seemed like a lifetime only to take a wasted voyage? Many of the new immigrants found Ellis Island more frightening than the ocean crossing.

One New York journalist described the first day at Ellis Island. "The day of the immigrants' arrival in New York was the nearest earthly likeness to the final day of judgment, when we have to prove our fitness to enter Heaven."

When the ferryboat docked at the island, the immigrants were herded off the boat and into one of the red brick buildings. Guards shouted, "Hurry up now. Quit poking around. We haven't got all day." The center at Ellis Island was built to handle five thousand people daily. During the high tide of immigration more than twice that number passed through the main hall each day.

*Immigrants arriving at Ellis Island*

*After climbing a stairway (left) to reach the Registry Room, new arrivals were given numbered identification tags (right).*

Guards tied large tags to the immigrants' coats. Each tag had a number on it. At the end of a long hallway, these numbers were shouted out in Italian, Yiddish, Greek, Croatian, Polish, German, and other languages. After much pushing and shouting, the newcomers were separated into groups of thirty. Then the bewildered immigrants were taken to the Registry Room. It was the largest room many of them had ever seen. A maze of aisles crisscrossed the room. Long lines of people stood in these aisles waiting to be examined by doctors or

*In the huge room known as the Registry Room, immigrants waited
to be examined by doctors and questioned by immigration officials.*

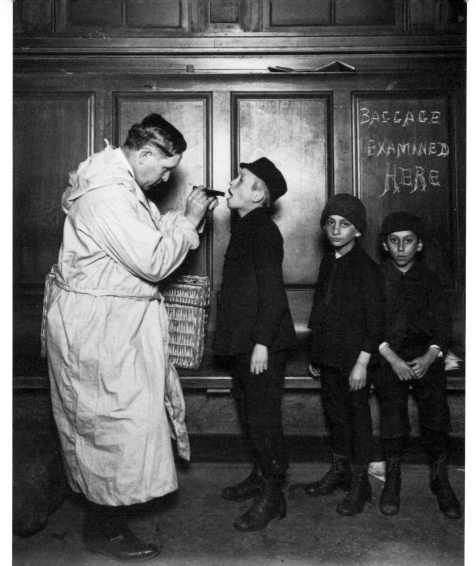

questioned by immigration officers. The noise
inside was a din of shouts, curses, and crying
children.

First came the doctors. Children over the age
of two were made to walk to see if they had a
limp. People were checked carefully by doctors.
Each doctor held a piece of chalk. If a doctor
suspected a heart problem, he would write a
giant H on the immigrant's coat. That immigrant

would then be sent to another room to wait for a more thorough examination. Other letters were chalked onto coats. F meant facial rash, Sc meant scalp infection, K meant hernia. The most dreaded letter of all was X. That meant mental problems, and people marked with an X were usually sent right back where they came from.

After the doctors, came the questions of an immigration officer. "What kind of work do you do? Can you read and write? How much money do you have? Have you ever been in prison?"

Immigration laws were confusing, and they kept changing. For example, new immigrants were told by relatives who had already been through Ellis Island to say "no" when asked if

*More than half of the immigrants entering the United States between 1898 and 1924 passed through Ellis Island's gates.*

they had a job waiting. "But wouldn't it sound better if I said I had a job in the United States?" the immigrant wondered. The answer was no. Having a job before entering the country broke the 1885 contract labor law passed by Congress.

About one in six immigrants was kept at Ellis Island for medical or other reasons. Those held were given hearings and further medical examinations. They could remain on the island for as long as four days. Most would finally be allowed to immigrate. But about 2 percent of the people were sent back to Europe.

*Those who were detained on the island were given simple but filling meals, such as soup or a thick stew.*

*A small outdoor playground helped pass the time for children detained on the island.*

The dejection felt by those sent back was dreadful. Some, in desperation, tried to swim to the mainland. Most of them drowned. It is hard to imagine the suffering felt by parents who were told that three of their four children could enter America, but their fourth could not for medical reasons. Family groups were sometimes split up at Ellis Island, and children as young as ten years old were sent back to Europe alone.

An Italian American who worked at Ellis Island as an interpreter once said, "I never managed during the years I worked there to become callous to the mental anguish, the disappointment, and the despair I witnessed

*Immigrants leaving Ellis Island*

*Fiorello La Guardia*

daily. . . . At best the work was an ordeal." That man would later become a famous mayor of New York City. His name was Fiorello La Guardia.

If an immigrant passed all his tests, his stay on Ellis Island lasted only about five hours. But to him the experience remained one that he would talk about for the rest of his life.

When the last question was asked and the last doctor satisfied, the immigrant was shown out of the Registry Room. He walked down a hall to a door that was labeled, curiously, PUSH TO NEW YORK. He pushed.

After a ferryboat ride, the immigrant found himself in the middle of New York City. It was baffling and fearsome. Yet in many ways it was the most exciting place he had ever seen. The buildings seemed to tower higher than mountains. One immigrant wondered why there was no snow on the top of them. Never had the newcomer from Europe seen so much traffic. Streetcars clanged down the streets. At every corner the new immigrant discovered something he had never seen before. A Polish woman wrote home, "On my first day in New York I saw both a Chinese man and a Negro woman. I knew then that I was in America." A Russian wrote, "On my first day I ate a sticky white fruit. I liked it. It was called a *panana.*"

The very first obstacle many immigrants faced was the English language. Most of them had addresses of friends or relatives, but they could not say where they wanted to go. A German hoped to go to "Linkinbra." He meant Lincoln, Nebraska. A Hungarian woman became angry when no one could understand that she wanted to go to "Szekenevo, Pillsburs." She meant Second Avenue, Pittsburgh. A young Polish immigrant had borrowed an English book while on board ship. He had practiced these words over and over again, "Can you direct me to the nearest Yumka? Can you direct me to the nearest Yumka?" He wanted to go to the nearest YMCA.

Many carefully thought-out plans collapsed on that first day in New York City. One family with nine children left Ellis Island with just a few dollars. They were not worried because Uncle Otto from the old country was to meet them in New York with train tickets to Cleveland. The money for the tickets had been sent six months earlier. The family waited and waited. Uncle Otto never showed up.

Many immigrants stayed in New York. Soon that city had the most varied population on earth. By 1920, New York held more Italians than Rome, more Germans than Bremen, and more Irish than Dublin. It had more Jewish people than any other city in the world.

Other immigrants scattered about the country. Most went to big cities where they could find jobs. There they gathered in neighborhoods, turning them into little Italys, little Polands, and little Germanys. They read newspapers printed in their own languages. They shopped at stores that sold food from their old countries.

Neighborhoods set up by the new immigrants often resembled the boundary lines of old Europe. One man wrote about Chicago: "On a summer day when the windows were open you could close your eyes and still tell what neighborhood you were in. All you had to do was smell the cooking and figure out if it was Polish, Italian, German, or Jewish."

*Many eastern European immigrants who passed through Ellis Island settled on New York's Lower East Side.*

It took several years for the new immigrant to adjust to life in America. The first few years were the loneliest. "It is true I have work and I'm not hungry. But I have not laughed since I came to America," wrote one Greek woman. A Russian wrote a long letter to his aunt telling her how much he missed his old village, but ended his letter with these words: "But I will not go back if someone was to give me the master's estate. Once you have tasted America there is no way to go back to those old miseries."

The mass movement of people from eastern and southern Europe to the United States changed the character of the country forever. No longer were the majority of the American people from northern Europe or the British Isles. Writer Robert Benchley once said of the United States, "We call England the mother country, but most of us come from Poland or Italy."

The United States was called the "Great Melting Pot" during those years when European immigrants flocked to her shores. In most cases, the immigrants preferred to live alongside people from their mother country. But their children blended together easily. Poles, Germans, Jews, and Italians all went to the same schools. In Europe they might have been enemies, but in the United States they played together. The children also learned English faster than did their parents and were quicker to adopt American ways.

Eventually, the adults adopted American ways also. A few even changed their names to make them sound more American.

The immigrants came to the United States, worked, and obeyed the laws. But as their numbers grew, so did their enemies.

Organized labor had always been against allowing so many thousands of newcomers to enter the country. The unions said the immigrants were holding down wages. The charge was largely true. The immigrant had to take whatever job he could get, and big business knew it. Around the time of World War I, labor

*Most immigrants who settled in the big cities initially worked long hours for little pay (right). Their children attended school with children of many other immigrant groups (left).*

unions became more powerful. They pressured Congress to limit immigration.

In the East, groups spoke out against immigration. They claimed that the newcomers from eastern and southern Europe were "destroying the purity of the American race." The Ku Klux Klan also wanted to stop immigration. They disliked the new arrivals because most of them were either Catholic or Jewish. Responding to these pressures, Congress passed a new immigration law in 1921. It not only limited the number of immigrants allowed in the country, but also set up a quota system. Under the new law, each country was given a quota, a fixed number of people that would be allowed to immigrate. The quota system put strict limits on countries in southern and eastern Europe.

The new law was effective. The flood of immigrants entering the country during the 1900s and 1910s slowed down to a trickle during the 1920s and 1930s. The golden gate at Ellis Island was swinging shut.

Today it is hard to understand why the immigrant was so disliked and feared by many native-born Americans. The men and women who arrived at Ellis Island in the late 1800s and early 1900s became the most productive Americans of the twentieth century. Their labor made the steel that forged modern America. Their muscle built the great cities. And their sons and daughters became the doctors, lawyers, business people, and politicians who later led the country.

The immigrants came, asking only for a chance. They brought with them a willingness to work hard and a hunger for learning. For many years, the United States has been the envy of the world, thanks largely to the contributions of those hopeful immigrants who once passed through Ellis Island.

Ellis Island closed as an immigration center in 1954. Slowly thereafter, the buildings fell into ruin. The enormous Registry Room, where frightened immigrants had been herded past doctors and officials, became a graveyard of overturned desks and rusting file cabinets. But in the hearts of immigrants and their children and grandchildren, Ellis Island remained a golden door that had ushered them into a new and prosperous life. Surely the island's facilities deserved a better fate than neglect.

In 1984, work began on a $160 million restoration project designed to turn Ellis Island into a museum celebrating the immigrant experience. A small army of workers poured onto the island and carefully restored the Registry Room to look as it did more than a half century earlier when it received thousands of immigrants each day. The work at Ellis Island was the most expensive restoration project ever undertaken in America. Much of the cost was met by the grateful descendants of immigrant families.

*The Registry Room before (left) and after (right) restoration*

*In 1990, the main building at Ellis Island reopened as the Ellis Island Immigration Museum.*

The Ellis Island Immigration Museum opened on September 10, 1990. Today, the Registry Room greets curious visitors instead of bewildered immigrants. Many of the museum guests have personal ties to Ellis Island. It is estimated that 40 percent of all Americans have a direct ancestor who was once processed through the island's facilities. On the museum walls are haunting black-and-white pictures of immigrants being examined by doctors while they move slowly through long lines. A visitor can imagine

*The restoration of Ellis Island was the most expensive project of its kind in American history.*

their fears as well as experience their joy when the last grueling exam was finished. During the long ocean passage and the frightening five-hour trial at Ellis Island, the immigrant yearned to begin his new life in the new country. The lucky ones finally saw the door that said, PUSH TO NEW YORK. They pushed. And they built America.

## INDEX

## PHOTO CREDITS

Cover, The Bettmann Archive; 1, 2, UPI/Bettmann Newsphotos; 3, Lewis W. Hine Collection/The New York Public Library; 4, Photri; 5, The Bettmann Archive; 7 (two pictures), Courtesy of the The New-York Historical Society, New York; 9, 10, The Bettmann Archive; 11, AP/Wide World Photos; 12, The Bettmann Archive; 13, 14, Photri; 15, The Bettmann Archive; 16 (two pictures), 17, Lewis W. Hine Collection/The New York Public Library; 18, The Bettmann Archive; 19, 20, AP/Wide World Photos; 21, Lewis W. Hine Collection/The New York Public Library; 22 (top), The Bettmann Archive; 22 (left), 25, 27 (left), AP/Wide World Photos; 27 (right), The Bettmann Archive; 29 (left), © 1987 Nick Cerulli; 29 (right), © Jon Riley/Tony Stone Worldwide/Chicago LTD.; 30 (left), © Dave Forbert; 30 (right), © Jon Riley/Tony Stone Worldwide/Chicago LTD.; 31, © Dave Forbert

Picture Identifications:
Cover: Italian immigrants at Ellis Island in 1905
Page 1: A family viewing the Manhattan skyline from Ellis Island
Page 2: A 1915 photograph of newly arrived immigrants on shipboard

Project Editor: Shari Joffe
Designer: Karen Yops
Cornerstones of Freedom Logo: David Cunningham

## ABOUT THE AUTHOR

**Mr. Stein** visited Ellis Island shortly after the new museum opened. He was one of the many museum guests who had close ties to the island. His mother immigrated through Ellis Island when she was a little girl. She is the Croatian woman quoted in this book.

R. Conrad Stein was born and raised in a Chicago neighborhood that was composed largely of European immigrants who had fresh memories of their Atlantic passage and their ordeal at Ellis Island. Mr. Stein has written many other books, articles, and short stories for young readers. He lives in Chicago with his wife and their daughter Janna.